TO: Dad

FROM: Ricky

DATE: 6/27/02

AARON BARKER

Introduction by George Strait

Love Without End, *Amen*

RUTLEDGE HILL PRESS®
NASHVILLE, TENNESSEE

A Division of Thomas Nelson, Inc.
www.ThomasNelson.com

Published by Rutledge Hill Press, a division of Thomas Nelson, Inc., P.O. Box 141000, Nashville, Tennessee 37214.

Design: Lookout Design Group, Inc., Minneapolis, Mn

Photos of George Strait on pages 7 and 9 by Mark Tucker.

Photo on page 44 © 2002 by Vicki Kasala / Image Bank

ISBN: 1-55853-971-9

Printed in the United States of America

02 03 04 05 06 — 5 4 3 2 1

Love Without End, *Amen*

I got sent home from school one day
    with a shiner on my eye.
Fightin' was against the rules and
    it didn't matter why.
When Dad got home I told that story
    just like I'd rehearsed.
Then stood there on those tremblin'
    knees and waited for the worst.

He said, "Let me tell you a secret
    about a father's love,
A secret that my daddy said was just
    between us."
He said, "Daddies don't just love
    their children every now and then.

It's a love without end, amen.
It's a love without end, amen."

When I became a father in the spring
    of '81,
There was no doubt that stubborn boy
    was just like my father's son.
And when I thought my patience had
    been tested to the end,
I took my daddy's secret and passed
    it on to him.

I said,"Let me tell you a secret
    about a father's love,
A secret that my daddy said was just
    between us."
I said, "Daddies don't just love
    their children every now and then.

It's a love without end, amen.
It's a love without end, amen."

Last night I dreamed I died and stood
    outside those pearly gates,
When suddenly I realized there must be
    some mistake.
If they know half the things I've done,
    they'll never let me in.
Then somewhere from the other side, I
    heard these words again.

They said, "Let me tell you a secret
    about a father's love,
A secret that my daddy said was just
    between us.
You see, daddies don't just love their
    children every now and then.

It's a love without end, amen.
It's a love without end, amen."

"Love Without End, Amen"
is a very special song to me.

When Aaron Barker first brought it to me,
I was touched by the simple
yet profound message that it sent.

A parent's love for a child is truly unconditional.

I can remember growing up and learning
a healthy respect for my father's authority,
but also appreciating his love and understanding,
even when I didn't feel like I deserved it.

Many of the lessons that he tried to instill
in me over the years became abundantly clear
when I was introduced to fatherhood.

I LOOK FORWARD

To what the future might bring

I have received many notes and letters from fans
describing what this song has meant to them
and about how it has affected their lives.

I must say that it has been as rewarding for me
as it has been for them.
I have been very fortunate to share many
wonderful moments with my son and
eagerly look forward to what the future might bring.

I sincerely hope that he will have
the opportunity to experience the
indescribable feeling that
unconditional love for a child brings.

It truly is a "Love Without End, Amen."

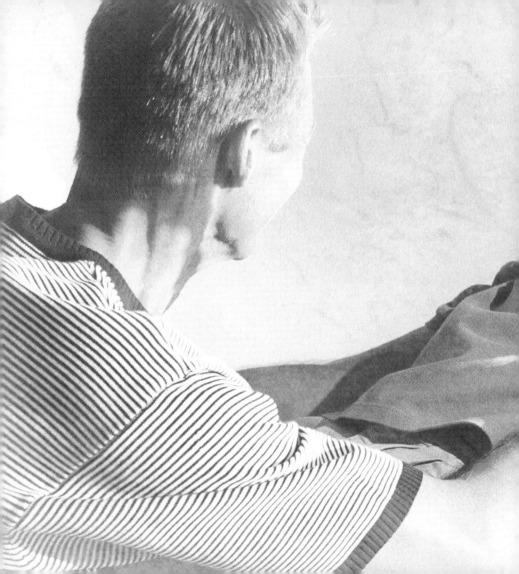

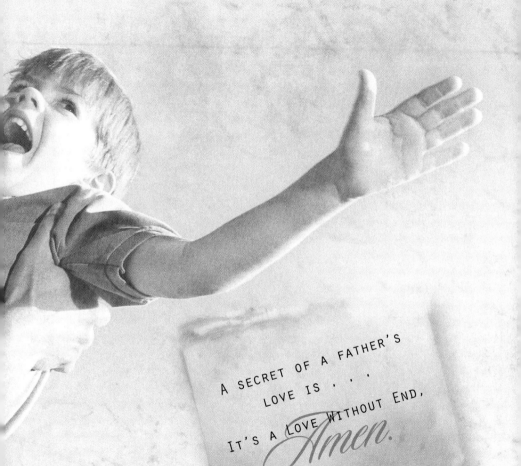

I GOT SENT HOME FROM
SCHOOL ONE DAY WITH
A SHINER ON MY EYE.

FIGHTIN' WAS AGAINST
THE RULES AND IT
DIDN'T MATTER WHY.

WHEN DAD GOT HOME
I TOLD THAT STORY
JUST LIKE I'D REHEARSED.

THEN STOOD THERE ON
THOSE TREMBLIN' KNEES
AND WAITED FOR THE WORST.

HE SAID . . .

"LET ME TELL
YOU A SECRET . . .

Whether by choice or chance,

I'M GLAD THAT YOU'RE MY DAD.

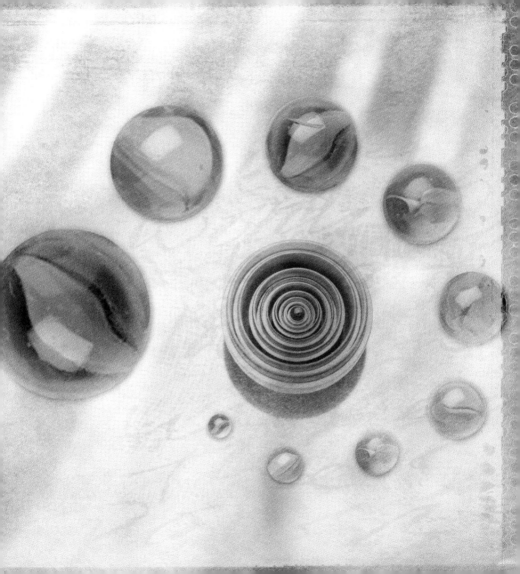

In the beginning I was like a stream

And you were like the banks of a river.

As I grew, I became like a river

And YOU WERE THERE *to show me the way.*

There were times I ran off course

And YOU WERE THERE

to guide me back.

I ran quickly and anxiously to see what was ahead

And you did your best to teach me to slow down

And appreciate what was here now.

Always in a hurry, I often crashed

into the banks of that river,

But you never faltered.

Each mile of my journey I would carry a little more of you with me,

SLOWLY LEARNING

YOUR WISDOM,

YOUR PATIENCE,

AND YOUR STRENGTH.

Each day I learned to run a little slower
and to appreciate the present.

And now, if you look carefully
when I stand perfectly still,

You will see a
perfect reflection of you
. . . in me.

ABOUT A
FATHER'S LOVE,

Love is taught . . .

Love is learned . . .

Love is given . . .

THEN LOVE IS RETURNED . . .

A SECRET THAT
MY DADDY SAID
WAS JUST
BETWEEN US."

I was always happy
when you got home

And never felt safer
than when you
hugged me.

I always hoped that
someday I would be
as tall as you,

But I was never

TALLER

than when you
let me ride on
your shoulders.

You asked

I was always disappointed when I let you down,

But never closer to you than

when you said that you make mistakes too.

I always hoped that I could go with you,

And never prouder than

when you asked me to come along.

I was always sure that you loved me,

But never more certain than when you said it.

me to come along

He said, "Daddies don't just love their children every now and then.

WISDOM, UNDERSTANDING,
PATIENCE, COMPASSION,
AND FORGIVENESS . . .

These are the virtues of a father

Passed down from generation to generation

Like a treasured pocket watch from father to son to son.

IT'S A LOVE

WITHOUT

END,

Amen"

When I became a father
in the spring of '81,
There was no doubt
that stubborn boy was just
like my father's son.
And when I thought
my patience had been
tested to the end,
I took my daddy's secret
and passed it on to him.

I said . . .

"LET ME TELL
YOU A SECRET

B ECOMING A FATHER *is easy.*

The difficulty is in BEING ONE.

ABOUT A
FATHER'S LOVE,

There is a love that
can only be known
When waiting to welcome
a child of your own —

THE FEELINGS OF
WONDER, AND
WORRY, AND JOY,

Not caring if this one's
a girl or a boy,
Just hoping you're worthy
of something so dear
AND LOVING
THEM EVEN BEFORE
THEY ARE HERE.

A SECRET THAT MY DADDY
SAID WAS JUST BETWEEN US."

Take my hand and walk with me.

TELL ME OF YOUR DREAMS

And I will share the things with you

my father shared with me.

Follow in my footsteps

each step along the way.

I know the path you're walking now

'Cause I walked it yesterday.

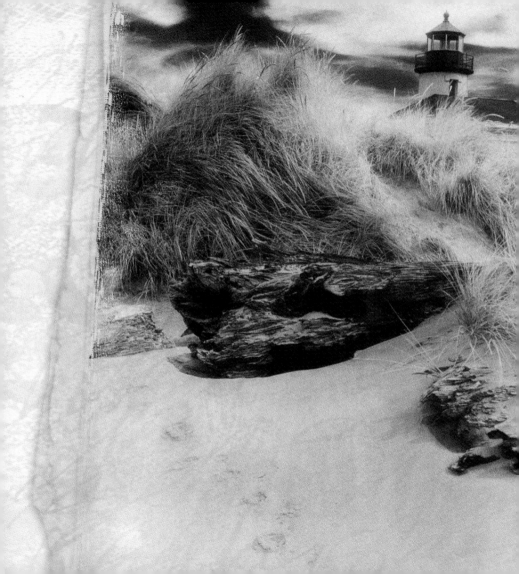

And if you choose to venture out

On pathways of your own,

Remember, Son, where love's concerned

YOU'LL NEVER WALK ALONE.

And most of all remember this:

No matter what you do,

My love is unconditional

And love *will see us through.*

I SAID, "DADDIES DON'T JUST LOVE THEIR CHILDREN EVERY NOW AND THEN.

Cherish your childhood and look at each day
Like a colorful float in a passing parade.

Be aware of the wonders of being a child,
Where unbridled dreams are allowed
    to run wild,

Where sidewalks and driveways
    are tricycle highways,
And dishtowels are superman capes,

Where seesaws and swings are like
    flying machines

And the world is a magical place.

'Cause one by one the days fly by

    Faster than fence posts on an afternoon drive—

From laughing and crying and learning to talk

    To learning to stand and then learning to walk.

And soon you will march to a whole different drum,

Not questioning once where the beat's coming from.

And a new generation begins its crusade

to the echo of drums from the passing parade.

IT'S A

LOVE

WITHOUT

END,

LAST NIGHT I DREAMED I DIED AND
STOOD OUTSIDE THOSE PEARLY GATES,
WHEN SUDDENLY I REALIZED THERE
MUST BE SOME MISTAKE.

IF THEY KNOW HALF THE THINGS
I'VE DONE, THEY'LL NEVER LET ME IN.
THEN SOMEWHERE FROM THE OTHER SIDE,
I HEARD THESE WORDS AGAIN.

THEY SAID · · ·

"LET ME TELL
YOU A SECRET

The years come and go, but the memories last

      Like a life-long collection of old photographs.

We slowly go over the days one by one

      And evaluate everything, all that we've done.

Memories remind us that time marches on

And carries us with it, . . . but we take along

The memories of times
that were simple and good.

As well as those things we would change if we could.

So keep this in mind

as you look to the past

To answer the questions

that everyone asks:

HAS MY LIFE

MADE A DIFFERENCE

TO ANYONE HERE?

DOES MY LIFE

HAVE A PURPOSE?

. . . The answer is clear.

GOD *has a reason for all He creates.*

And remember that HEAVEN

does not make mistakes.

ABOUT A FATHER'S LOVE,

When you wonder if God
understands your mistakes,
Will heaven forgive you
and open its gates,

Remember the love
that you felt for your child.
The first time you held him,
the first time he smiled.

Now think about that
and then ask yourself this:
Would your father in heaven
love you any less?

These things will help
you to realize too
That God's love is a gift
sent from heaven to you.

And then you can know
the true meaning of
unending and pure

unconditional
LOVE.

A SECRET THAT MY DADDY
SAID WAS JUST BETWEEN US.

Life is a gift,

an adventure to live,

THE MOST PRECIOUS GIFT

that a father can give.

Don't ever mistake it

for something it's not,

And live every day like

it's all that you've got.

So, let me tell you a secret,

The one my father told,

The story of a Father's love

A long, long time ago—

A love so great He gave His Son

That we might live again.

The secret of a Father's love is . . .

IT'S A LOVE WITHOUT END . . .

Amen.

You see, daddies don't just love their children every now and then.

LOVE

does not begin . . .

LOVE

does not end . . .

LOVE

just is . . .

IT'S A LOVE WITHOUT END, *Amen."*

Thanks
DAD *for loving me!*